**W9-AMN-244**

# Journalist

# CAREERS WITH CHARACTER

CAREERS WITH CHARACTER

# Journalist

Sherry Bonnice

Mason Crest

Mason Crest
450 Parkway Drive, Suite D
Broomall, PA 19008
www.masoncrest.com

Printed in the Hashemite Kingdom of Jordan.

First printing
9 8 7 6 5 4 3 2 1

Series ISBN: 978-1-4222-2750-3
ISBN: 978-1-4222-2758-9
ebook ISBN: 978-1-4222-9054-5

The Library of Congress has cataloged the
    hardcopy format(s) as follows:

Library of Congress Cataloging-in-Publication Data

Bonnice, Sherry, 1956-
  [Journalism]
  Journalist / Sherry Bonnice.
      pages cm. – (Careers with character)
  Includes index.
  Originally published under title: Journalism.
  ISBN 978-1-4222-2758-9 (hardcover) – ISBN 978-1-4222-2750-3 (series) – ISBN 978-1-4222-9054-5
(ebook)
  1. Journalism-Juvenile literature. 2. Journalism-Vocational guidance-Juvenile literature. I. Title.
  PN4776.B64 2014
  070.4'023–dc23
                    2013007510

Produced by Vestal Creative Services.
www.vestalcreative.com

Photo Credits:
Artville: pp. 23, 54
Digital Stock: pp. 10, 18, 70, 88
Dover, Dictionary of American Portraits: pp. 32, 36, 43, 69, 84
PhotoDisc: pp. 14, 22, 26, 40, 71, 79, 86
PhotoSpin: pp. 35, 82
Reuters: pp. 12, 50, 58, 60, 61, 62, 74, 76
Viola Ruelke Gommer: pp. 42, 52, 55

# CONTENTS

*We each leave a fingerprint on the world.*
*Our careers are the work we do in life.*
*Our characters are shaped by the choices*
*we make to do good.*
*When we combine careers with character,*
*we touch the world with power.*

# INTRODUCTION

by Dr. Cheryl Gholar
and Dr. Ernestine G. Riggs

In today's world, the awesome task of choosing or staying in a career has become more involved than one would ever have imagined in past decades. Whether the job market is robust or the demand for workers is sluggish, the need for top-performing employees with good character remains a priority on most employers' lists of "must have" or "must keep." When critical decisions are being made regarding a company or organization's growth or future, job performance and work ethic are often the determining factors as to who will remain employed and who will not.

How does one achieve success in one's career and in life? Victor Frankl, the Austrian psychologist, summarized the concept of success in the preface to his book *Man's Search for Meaning* as: "The unintended side-effect of one's personal dedication to a course greater than oneself." Achieving value by responding to life and careers from higher levels of knowing and being is a specific goal of teaching and learning in "Careers with Character." What constitutes success for us as individuals can be found deep within our belief system. Seeking, preparing, and attaining an excellent career that aligns with our personality is an outstanding goal. However, an excellent career augmented by exemplary character is a visible expression of the human need to bring meaning, purpose, and value to our work.

Career education informs us of employment opportunities, occupational outlooks, earnings, and preparation needed to perform certain tasks. Character education provides insight into how a person of good character might choose to respond, initiate an action, or perform specific tasks in the presence of an ethical dilemma. "Careers with Character" combines the two and teaches students that careers are more than just jobs. Career development is incomplete without character development. What better way to explore careers and character than to make them a single package to be opened, examined, and reflected upon as a means of understanding the greater whole of who we are and what work can mean when one chooses to become an employee of character?

*Character* can be defined simply as "who you are even when no one else is around." Your character is revealed by your choices and actions. These bear your personal signature, validating the story of who you are. They are the fingerprints you leave behind on the people you meet and know; they are the ideas you bring into reality. Your choices tell the world what you truly believe.

Character, when viewed as a standard of excellence, reminds us to ask ourselves when choosing a career: "Why this particular career, for what purpose, and to what end?" The authors of "Careers with Character" knowledgeably and passionately, through their various vignettes, enable one to experience an inner journey that is both intellectual and moral. Students will find themselves, when confronting decisions in real life, more prepared, having had experiential learning opportunities through this series. The books, however, do not separate or negate the individual good from the academic skills or intellect needed to perform the required tasks that lead to productive career development and personal fulfillment.

Each book is replete with exemplary role models, practical strategies, instructional tools, and applications. In each volume, individuals of character work toward ethical leadership, learning how to respond appropriately to issues of not only right versus wrong, but issues of right versus right, understanding the possible benefits and consequences of their decisions. A wealth of examples is provided.

What is it about a career that moves our hearts and minds toward fulfilling a dream? It is our character. The truest approach to finding out who we are and what illuminates our lives is to look within. At the very heart of career development is good character. At the heart of good character is an individual who knows and loves the good, and seeks to share the good with others. By exploring careers and character together, we create internal and external environments that support and enhance each other, challenging students to lead conscious lives of personal quality and true richness every day.

Is there a difference between doing the right thing, and doing things right? Career questions ask, "What do you know about a specific career?" Character questions ask, "Now that you know about a specific career, what will you choose to do with what you know?" "How will you perform certain tasks and services for others, even when no one else is around?" "Will all individuals be given your best regardless of their socioeconomic background, physical condition, ethnicity, or religious beliefs?" Character questions often challenge the authenticity of what we say we believe and value in the workplace and in our personal lives.

Character and career questions together challenge us to pay attention to our lives and not fall asleep on the job. Career knowledge, self-knowledge, and ethical wisdom help us answer deeper questions about the meaning of work; they give us permission to transform our lives. Personal integrity is the price of admission.

The insight of one "ordinary" individual can make a difference in the world—if that one individual believes that character is an amazing gift to uncap knowledge and talents to empower the human community. Our world needs everyday heroes in the workplace—and "Careers with Character" challenges students to become those heroes.

Like Clark Kent, Superman's mild-mannered disguise, real-life journalists stand for truth and justice.

# JOB REQUIREMENTS

*Undertaking the responsibility to inform the public of important news issues is an awesome task that requires an ethics-based respect for everyone concerned.*

# CHAPTER ONE

Almost everyone has heard of Clark Kent, the mild-mannered reporter who worked for the *Daily Planet* in Metropolis. He covered news events and changed into his Superman costume whenever he was needed to fight for "truth, justice, and the American way." Together with his fellow employees, reporter Lois Lane and photographer Jimmy Olsen, his goal was to report the news for the citizens of Metropolis.

Although Clark Kent and his fellow workers were not real characters, they did portray an accurate picture of what journalists do when they work as reporters for a newspaper. Just like their real-world counterparts, their job was to investigate news events and

12

quickly write about them before a deadline. What's more, Clark, both as a reporter and as a superhero, cared for those he served.

Similarly, reporters now and throughout history have made an impact on those around them with their commitment to expose the truth, no matter the cost. Journalism offers an opportunity to serve with integrity and truth, to show respect and compassion for those whose stories you report and those who will gain the knowledge you share. News reporters give to the world insights that challenge and awaken; they help destroy biased points of view.

Present-day reporters, like Barbara Walters, often report on diffi- cult issues. Walters, who paved the way for women in television me- dia reporting, worked her way from news writer to reporter, inter- viewer, editor, and writer. Eventually she became a host on NBC's highly rated *Today Show*. Walters has traveled around the world, earning stories and personal profiles, including interviews with United States presidents and foreign leaders such as Anwar Sadat, Muammar Qaddafi, and Fidel Castro. She accompanied the NBC

Barbara Walters uses her journalistic skills to interview former President George W. Bush on his ranch in Texas.

team to China to cover the visits of President Richard Nixon in 1972 and President Gerald Ford in 1975. Walters received a degree from Sarah Lawrence College but did not graduate anticipating a career in journalism. She excelled in English and creative writing, and although she did not prepare specifically to become a reporter, her love of the written word and a desire to know the truth about situations and people led her to a successful career.

If you are interested in journalism, you can begin by enrolling in any journalism courses offered at your high school. Check with your school's guidance counselor, who can help put together the best courses designed for college-bound students. You will need four years of English, in addition to courses in history, sciences, social studies, math, and more. Volunteer to work on the school newspaper or magazine.

Once enrolled in college, earning a bachelor's degree in journalism is the most obvious route to employment. But, like Walters, you may be hired even if you have another major. Most employers require experience as well as education. Working on college newspapers or interning with news organizations is helpful. Some large city newspapers and radio or television stations require degrees in specific subjects. Economics, business, and political science are a few such majors.

## Career Options for Journalists

If you are interested in a career as a journalist, you have many areas from which to choose. Here are some of the most common careers for journalists:

- News Reporter
- Editor
- Copyeditor
- Investigative Reporter
- Magazine Writer
- Magazine Editor
- **Freelance Writer**
- Foreign Correspondent
- Speech Writer
- **Ghostwriter**

# 14

Keeping a journal is a good technique for improving your writing skills.

### Exercises to Help You Become a Better Journalist

You can do some things while you are still in school that will help you become a better journalist. These include:

- Keeping a journal—and writing in it every day. This will help you practice your writing skills and learn to put your thoughts together.
- Reading. Good writers are also good readers, so read every day. The newspaper, magazines, and Internet should be on your daily reading schedule, as well as books, both fiction and nonfiction.
- Attending a workshop or a writers' conference. You will gain valuable information and meet people who make their living writing. They can share some of their experiences.

Some of the classes involved in a journalism major are basic reporting, *copyediting*, history of journalism, and press law and *ethics*. With the advent of online journalism, those who specialize in computer skills are able to use traditional reporting methods along with audio and video elements to create a new kind of journalism. Students may continue their education to earn a master's degree and a Ph.D. in journalism.

In addition to the educational requirements, journalists must have integrity, trustworthiness, self-discipline, and respect for people. Without these character traits, a free-press society does not help those it serves.

The right to free speech is something that our forefathers worked hard to protect. They considered it so important that the First Amendment of the U.S. Constitution reads, "Congress shall make no law respecting an establishment of religion, or prohibiting the free exercise thereof; or abridging the freedom of speech, or of the press;

The invention of the printing press meant that news and ideas could be quickly shared across an entire community.

or the right of the people peaceably to assemble, and to petition the Government for a redress of grievances." Through the ratification of the Bill of Rights in 1791, these principles of free press and free speech became part of the American heritage. In Canada, a similar document guarantees to Canadians "the liberties of an open society with a free and vigorous press."

Ever since the invention of the printing press, journalists have worked hard to communicate information to their readers. Throughout history, newspapers have been successful because they provided a valuable service to the public. From Benjamin Franklin, who in 1729 established a newspaper called the *Pennsylvania Gazette*, to the Gannett chain, which consists of more than 80 newspapers and is best known for *USA Today*, newspapers have provided journalists with many job opportunities.

Many people choose a career in journalism because they have a curious mind. They are always asking questions, and want to get to the truth. Journalists have a spirit that recognizes the wealth and depth of information in our world. In addition, they know how to turn that information into news stories, books, magazine articles, and other forms of communication to make it interesting to the public. A journalist must also earn the respect and trust of her colleagues and the people about whom she will be writing. She must have the courage to go after the truth and the integrity to protect her sources. At times she may find it more difficult to remain unbiased. Other times a reporter may find himself with many antagonists and few persons who see the evidence as he does. At such times diligence and self-discipline may reward him with an article that proves the facts and reveals the truth.

These are all reasons why a good character is an essential requirement for journalism. According to character education expert Dr. Thomas Lickona, good character depends on possessing certain core values. Journalists must practice these values as they deal with people and report the news. Dr. Lickona believes that values must be passed on by adults to the next generation. We each have the responsibility to keep the foundations of our society intact. Journalists do this when they make a deliberate effort to share values and educate the public with responsible news stories.

In the chapters that follow we will look at the lives of some journalists who have had an impact on society. The field of journalism embodies many examples of those who use their profession and talents to make a difference. They show through their work:

- integrity and trustworthiness
- respect and compassion
- justice and fairness
- responsibility
- courage
- self-discipline and diligence
- citizenship

When journalists demonstrate these qualities through their work, they help to create a better world for us all.

---

*To love what you do and feel that it matters—how could anything be more fun?*

—Katharine Graham

---

Integrity is as important as writing skills if you want to be a journalist.

# INTEGRITY AND TRUSTWORTHINESS

*Being a person with integrity means that even when deadlines are tight you remain honest and trustworthy.*

## CHAPTER TWO

Rick Browning, an editor at the daily newspaper in a city outside of Miami, Florida, considers himself an honest person. He has worked hard to gain the trust and respect of his bosses and his peers at the newspaper.

As the editor of the special weekly supplement known as "Crossroads," he is in charge of about a dozen local freelance writers. The freelance writers submit most of the articles written for "Crossroads," and Rick has gotten to know a few of them very well.

He likes working as the editor of the supplement because most of the articles are profiles of local people in the community. In one week's edition there might be interviews with a school librarian, a profile of a new business that has opened up in town, a story about a senior citizen who makes crafts in her spare time, or articles about local hobby clubs. Every week, Rick works hard to present a good representation of ordinary people who are doing their normal activities. He feels fortunate to have such a great bunch of freelance writers who each week contribute their stories on time.

Some of the writers have been working with Rick for the past five years, ever since he was named editor of the "Crossroads" section. For instance, Sue Walton, a retired newspaper reporter, likes to supplement her pension by writing a few freelance articles each month. Because of Sue's experience working at a newspaper in upstate New York, Rick never has to do much editing on any of the stories she files. Her work is always in on time, and she somehow manages to get great quotes to go along with each newspaper article she writes.

Another freelance writer, Ben Larkin, is a young man with no formal journalism training. However, Ben also manages to turn in some well-written articles, and although Rick has to spend more time editing Ben's stories, he is still pleased overall with Ben's performance. Secretly, however, Rick wishes he had more freelance writers like Sue Walton working for him. His job would be far easier and take much less time if all the writers had Sue's skills.

Ben recently had a problem completing a freelance assignment for "Crossroads." He had been scheduled to visit the local elementary school to interview three students who were selected to participate in a science program at the Smithsonian Institute in Washington, D.C. The principal had agreed to the interview, and Ben had contacted Rick to let him know what he was doing, and then made an appointment for a photographer to come out to the school to take pictures of the three students. But on the morning Ben was supposed to visit the school to interview the students, his car would not start. He called Rick and told him he would not be able to complete the article after all.

"Thanks for letting me know, Ben," Rick told the freelance writer. "I'll call one of the other freelancers and see if they can cover it for you." Rick knew whom he wanted for this assignment: Sue Walton would be perfect for the job. Her experience in writing newspaper stories, both when she was on staff and as a freelance contributor, would give this story the professional touch he wanted. When he called Sue, she agreed to go to the elementary school and take over the assignment from Ben.

As Rick hung up the telephone from talking with Sue, he breathed a sigh of relief. Now he would not have to worry about having a hole in next week's edition of "Crossroads." He knew he could count on Sue to get the interviews and turn in the story before the deadline later that evening.

A few hours later, Rick was feeling pretty good. He had all of the articles ready to go for next week's issue of "Crossroads," and he was just waiting for Sue Walton to file hers. When he returned from a short break, he found an email from Sue; just as he'd expected, the

People who value integrity and trustworthiness:

- tell the truth.
- don't withhold important information.
- are sincere; they don't deceive, mislead, or be devious and tricky.
- don't betray a trust.
- don't steal.
- don't cheat.
- stand up for beliefs about right and wrong.
- keep their promises.
- return what they have borrowed and pay their debts.
- stand by, support, and protect their families, friends, community, and country.
- don't talk behind people's backs or spread rumors.
- don't ask their friends to do something wrong.

Adapted from material from the Character Counts Coalition, character-counts.org/overview/about.html

story was in on time. After a quick read of her story, he knew it was perfect. It did not warrant any editing at all. And the quotes

**22**

An *ethical dilemma* is situation that demands we make a choice about what is the right thing to do. If we want to be people who value the qualities of good character, then we must take the time to sort out these ethical dilemmas carefully.

were great. *I don't know how she manages to get such wonderful quotes*, Rick said to himself. As he entered the last article into the computer, he breathed a sigh of contentment.

A few minutes later, however, Rick received an error message from the newspaper's software program. "Quotes Repeat" was flashing on his computer screen, indicating that one of the quotes in the new edition had been used on a previous occasion in the newspaper; this feature of the program made sure Rick and his writers didn't repeat themselves from edition to edition.

*That's odd*, Rick thought to himself. He pushed "clear," thinking he must have received the message in error. After all, he had

The computer and the telephone are two of the journalist's most frequently used tools.

One way to solve an ethical dilemma is to ask yourself: If your actions were being observed, how would you behave?

checked and double-checked all the quotes in each of the articles that were going to appear in the next issue of "Crossroads." However, as he tried to enter Sue's story again, he still kept getting that error message. He decided to look into the error report that the newspaper software program provided.

After reading it several times, he was shocked by what he saw. The same quotes used in an article written by Sue Walton more than 18 months ago appeared in the article she had just filed.

He could not believe what he was reading. But it was true. Sue Walton had broken one of journalism's most important rules: she had obviously fabricated quotes and used them in a news story. Being a trustworthy journalist means integrity and truthfulness are essential. When Sue Walton used quotes from one story in another one, she was being dishonest. Rick was furious.

What should he do? He was on a tight deadline, and he knew that if he did not override the error message and allow Sue Walton's

This letter and editorial first appeared in the *New York Sun* in 1897, over a hundred years ago, and was reprinted annually until 1949 when the paper went out of business. It is probably the most popular editorial ever written, and it demonstrates one journalist's sense of integrity. He lived up to a young girl's trust by answering a difficult question with care and sensitivity.

We take pleasure in answering thus prominently the communication below, expressing at the same time our great gratification that its faithful author is numbered among the friends of *The Sun*:

Dear Editor—
I am 8 years old. Some of my little friends say there is no Santa Claus. Papa says, "If you see it in The Sun, it's so." Please tell me the truth, is there a Santa Claus?
    —Virginia O'Hanlon, 115 West Ninety-fifth Street

Virginia, your little friends are wrong. They have been affected by the scepticism of a sceptical age. They do not believe except they see. They think that nothing can be which is not comprehensible by their little minds. All minds, Virginia, whether they be men's or children's, are little. In this great universe of ours, man is a mere insect, an ant, in his intellect as compared with the boundless world about him, as measured by the intelligence capable of grasping the whole truth and knowledge.
    Yes, Virginia, there is a Santa Claus. He exists as certainly as love and generosity and devotion exist, and you know that they abound and give to your life its highest beauty and joy. Alas! how dreary would be the world if there were no Santa Claus! It would be as dreary as if there were no Virginias. There would be no childlike faith then, no poetry,

no romance to make tolerable this existence. We should have no enjoyment, except in sense and sight. The external light with which childhood fills the world would be extinguished.

Not believe in Santa Claus! You might as well not believe in fairies. You might get your papa to have men to watch in all the chimneys on Christmas eve to catch Santa Claus, but even if you did not see Santa Claus coming down, what would that prove? Nobody sees Santa Claus, but that is no sign that there is no Santa Claus. The most real things in the world are those that neither children nor men can see. Did you ever see fairies dancing on the lawn? Of course not, but that's no proof that they are not there. Nobody can conceive or imagine all the wonders there are unseen and unseeable in the world.

You tear apart the baby's rattle and see what makes the noise inside, but there is a veil covering the unseen world which not the strongest men, nor even the united strength of all the strongest men that ever lived could tear apart. Only faith, poetry, love romance, can push aside that curtain and view and picture the supernal beauty and glory beyond. Is it all real? Ah, Virginia, in all this world there is nothing else real and abiding.

story to be published, he would have a large hole in his "Crossroads" section.

As Rick cooled down, he remembered that Sue had been assigned the story at the last minute; maybe she wasn't able to get new quotes for the story. *It's probably something she's never done before, and it will never happen again,"* he said to himself.

Rick was reluctant to go to his managing editor and report that one of his freelance writers had fabricated quotes for a newspaper story. But he knew Sue had done something wrong; while he wanted to protect her from being in trouble with the newspaper, he also knew he needed to protect himself and do the right thing.

It's important to make decisions based on integrity the first time around, since life seldom offers us the chance to use the "delete" button.

Should Rick simply hit the override key and allow the newspaper story to be printed? Should he protect Sue Walton, who was his friend and had years of experience as a journalist? Or should he pull the story, and report the incident to his managing editor?

Rick had run smack into one of the most difficult ethical dilemmas in the world: truth versus loyalty. He had to make a choice: should he tell the truth and report the incident to his managing editor? Or should he be loyal to a fellow journalist and protect her from the consequences of her actions?

Rushworth M. Kidder, the author of *How Good People Make Tough Choices*, writes that people often use three principles for resolving tough dilemmas like the one Rick faced. These principles are:

1.  Do what others want you to do. (This is referred to as "care-based" thinking.

2. Do what's best for the greatest number of people. (This is called "ends-based" thinking.)
3. Follow your highest sense of what is right. (This is called "rule-based" thinking.)

Rick used these principles as he struggled to sort out the situation. If he followed the care-based approach and did what others wanted him to do, then he supposed he would simply keep quiet and go on. That's what Sue Walton would want him to do, he was sure.

Everyone makes mistakes, he reasoned, especially when they have to do something at the last minute. Using ends-based thinking, he decided the best thing for himself, Sue Walton, and his managing editor would be to simply let the incident go.

### Three Foundations for Ethical Decision-Making

1. Take into account the interests and well-being of everyone concerned. (Don't do something that will help you if it will hurt another.)
2. When a character value like integrity and trustworthiness is at stake, always make the decision that will support that value. (For example, tell the truth even though it may cost you some embarrassment.)
3. Where two character values conflict (for instance, when telling the truth might hurt another person), choose the course of action that will lead to the greatest good for everyone concerned. Be sure to seek all possible alternatives, however; don't opt for dishonesty simply as the easiest and least painful way out of a difficult situation.

Adapted from materials from the Josephson Institute of Ethics, josephsoninstitute.org

# 28

However, when he tried to put the whole thing out of his mind, something still bothered his conscience. Somehow he did not feel honest if he failed to report the incident. Maybe he needed to use rule-based thinking and listen to his own personal sense of what was right.

What do you think Rick decided to do? What would you have done in his place?

*So long as we are able to distinguish any space whatever between truth and us we remain outside it.*

–Henri Amiel

By letting the world know the truth, journalists who write with respect and compassion can help bring about better living conditions' for the world's children.

# RESPECT AND COMPASSION

*When people possess respect and
compassion for others, they are willing
to take action to right a wrong.*

# CHAPTER THREE

Considered one of the best reporters in America during her lifetime, Nellie Bly (Elizabeth Cochrane Seaman) began her journalism career in 1885 at the age of 18. In her reply to an article in the *Pittsburgh Dispatch* titled "What Girls Are Good For," Nellie opposed the view that girls should stay at home and take care of babies, unconcerned about government or social issues. She told of the importance of her help in supporting her family after her father's death. Because of the well-written power of her response, the editor offered her a job.

Nellie's first assignment was as a stunt reporter. Stunt reporters did whatever necessary to get a story; she worked undercover at the

Copper Cable Factory. As Nellie worked, she witnessed the unfit conditions of the women and children employed there. She wrote about these conditions, hoping to bring about changes that would better the employees' lives. This was the beginning of a career filled with reporting on the injustices of women, children, and the poor. Nellie Bly made a difference in the lives of those she wrote about because she cared for the situations in which real people lived and worked.

In 1886, Nellie traveled through Mexico for six months. She reported on the corrupt government and poor living conditions of the people there. Although she was forced to leave the country, she had brought to her readers' attention the atrocities imposed on the poor by people with power and money.

Nellie Bly longed to help others through her writing in a larger arena, so in 1887 she went to New York City, hoping to work for the

Nellie Bly is an example of a compassionate journalist who used her writing skills to help others.

*New York World*. At the time there were very few female reporters, but Nellie knew the *World* covered social issues and had helped to expose corruption. She fought for a reporter's position and finally proved herself by pretending to be insane so she would be admitted into the New York Women's Lunatic Asylum.

Once there, she witnessed terrible abuse and mistreatment. The patients were fed moldy, stale food; they were bathed together in an open room with cold water. The nurses treated them harshly and sometimes even antagonized those who were most volatile. After ten days, Nellie was released by a lawyer from the *World*.

Show respect and compassion for others by:

1. being courteous and polite.
2. being open minded; accepting those who are a different race or religion.
3. assisting those who are mistreated by others.
4. sharing with others.
5. looking at a situation from the other person's perspective.
6. treating others as you want them to treat you.
7. forgiving others.

Adapted from material from the Character Counts Coalition, charactercounts.org/overview/about.html

The headline of Nellie Bly's story read:

BEHIND ASYLUM BARS
THE MYSTERY OF THE UNKNOWN INSANE GIRL
How Nellie Bly Deceived Judges, Reporters
and Medical Experts

A grand jury investigation into patient care followed her series of articles on the hospital. New York City's Department of Public Charities and Corrections gave a million-dollar increase in funding to the asylum. Nellie was paid handsomely for the article and was hired as

Long ago, the only written materials were created slowly and laboriously by hand; in today's computerized world, however, newspapers and magazines can be produced quickly, creating a society where news spreads almost instantly.

a full-time reporter. She continued to write about issues that helped expose wrongdoing.

Once, Nellie was imprisoned so that she could write about the conditions within women's jails. She also exposed a baby-selling ring when she pretended to be an unwed mother. But Nellie is probably most famous for her trip around the world. She traveled the world in less than 80 days to beat the record of Jules Verne's fictional character in *Around the World in Eighty Days*. She accomplished this feat and shared the stories with her readers.

During World War I, Nellie went to Europe and reported from

> Compassion is the ultimate and most meaningful embodiment of emotional maturity. It is through compassion that a person achieves the highest peak and deepest reach in his or her search for self-fulfillment.
> —Arthur Jersild

## The Associated Negro Press (ANP)

The ANP, founded in 1919 by Claude A. Barnett, was the oldest and largest African American press service in the United States. Barnett remained the director for more than 40 years as the ANP supplied news stories, opinion columns, feature essays, and reviews of books and movies to African American newspapers throughout the country. The members included nearly all the major African American newspapers in the United States. The news published by the ANP helped keep African Americans aware of the national and international news that particularly concerned them.

By reporting the facts, even when they are painful, journalists work to bring about a better world for children like this one.

the frontlines. She wrote about a soldier's life in a frontline trench. Finally, back in New York, Nellie used an advice column to match up orphans with foster parents. She raised one young girl herself.

Nellie Bly chose journalism as a career, but for her it was not just a means of making a living. Instead, she used her abilities to help others. Because of her compassion and intense hatred of social injustices, Nellie shared the truth about situations others would never have understood without her investigative work. Nellie affected the lives of the people she wrote about by exposing wrongdoings; she also enabled her readers to make a difference by showing them issues they could work to improve.

In an age when women were not considered capable of serious work, Nellie Bly's entire life provided an answer to that long-ago

Anne McCormick interviewed the great and famous people of her day, like President Harry Truman, and created news stories that made sense to ordinary folk.

## Timothy Thomas Fortune

One of the most powerful and influential African American editors of his time, T. Thomas Fortune began his journalist career as a typesetter. He then moved to the *New York Globe*, a large African American newspaper. Eventually, he worked for various papers, including the *Boston Transcript* and the *New York Sun*.

Fortune helped to organize the Afro-American League. One of the goals of the league was to create a positive public opinion through the writings of black Americans. The league worked toward:

- a healthy public opinion.
- an appeal to the courts of law for constitutional and legal rights.
- a peaceful and lawful process of accomplishing change.

Fortune never used the word "Negro" to refer to blacks; instead, he used "Afro American." Some believe he was the first to use the phrase.

editorial, "What Girls Are Good For." She showed everyone how powerful a woman can be, particularly a woman who lives with compassion and respect for others.

Anne O'Hare McCormick is another journalist who used her career to demonstrate her respect and compassion for others. In 1921, she sent a note to the managing editor of the *New York Times*, asking if she might send him some stories she wrote while in Europe on a business trip with her husband. This editor's positive response led McCormick to prove herself as a *stringer* for the newspaper. After 15 years, she was made the first woman to serve as a regular contributor to the editorial page of the *Times*. When she began,

McCormick was asked to be an editor who spoke about freedom; she would be the news reporter who would let readers know when freedom was challenged anywhere in the world. This was an awesome task, one which McCormick was able to handle.

Anne McCormick was known for her treatment of the news as it related to the everyday person. Based on this perspective, her insight into Mussolini's rise to power gained her great respect. In her interviews with Hitler, Stalin, Roosevelt, Truman, Eisenhower, and others, she showed that she cared greatly for how the news affected ordinary people. As she communicated with people she met in the streets wherever she went, McCormick treated them with the same esteem she showed to important figures. She was respected by both common people and world leaders.

At a time when the world was full of turmoil and change, McCormick offered her readers intelligent and compassionate columns that helped them understand the confusion of war. She earned a sizable following for her column and was greatly respected for her unbiased offerings of the news.

The first woman to receive a Pulitzer Prize for journalism, Anne McCormick earned the award in 1937 for foreign correspondence. She seemed always to be where the news was, giving her an opportunity to experience and then share news firsthand.

While Nellie Bly was able to bring about social changes with her aggressive style of investigating, Anne McCormick was able to gain insights into happenings during World War II and its surrounding history. Her readers were better able to cope with a world at war because of her ability to see the truth and relate it to her readers. She demonstrated her compassion and respect for her readers by writing in a way that helped them make sense of the world's frightening events.

In a similar way, Alice Allison Dunnigan became a herald of the injustices against African Americans. She was the chief of the Washington Bureau for the *Chicago Defender* in 1947, making her the first African American female correspondent with White House credentials. She covered Congress, the White House, the Supreme Court, and the State Department.

Dunnigan experienced racism first hand, even as she worked as a reporter. Once she was barred from covering one of President Eisenhower's speeches. At a senator's funeral, she had to sit with the servants in order to cover the event. Her tough questions to leading politicians made her both admired and feared, regardless of her race.

As a member of the Associated Negro Press, Dunnigan wrote on topics that concerned African Americans, including racism. Her compassion for her fellow African Americans led her to write aggressively about civil rights as she witnessed racism's consequences in business as well as politics. She helped open the journalistic field, especially in the Capital, for other African Americans, both men and women.

Journalists today show the same respect and compassion as that demonstrated by Nellie Bly, Anne McCormick, and Alice Allison Dunnigan. Whenever news reporters expose wrongdoing or report a difficult issue with sensitivity, they demonstrate their respect and compassion for others—and they help us all understand the world a little better. All too often, ignorance breeds hatred and violence, but understanding and knowledge have the power to build bridges of respect and compassion. These bridges cross the barriers that separate us from one another . . . and they build a better and more peaceful world.

---

*Compassion is the keen awareness of the interdependence of all things.*

—Thomas Merton

A journalist who is just and fair can change the world.

# JUSTICE
# AND FAIRNESS

*A commitment to justice sometimes causes conflict—but it makes our society better for everyone.*

# CHAPTER FOUR

da M. Tarbell learned at a young age that it was a privilege and even a duty to fight injustice in the world around her. Her father taught her that lesson as he fought against the South Improvement Company's takeover of the oil industry. Higher railroad shipping prices pushed independents like Ida Tarbell's father out of their livelihood. Because of John D. Rockefeller's alliance between three of the most powerful railroads and a few oil refiners, her father and other independents suffered enormous losses. Ida was only 15 years old at the time, and she had no idea then that she would influence the outcome of Rockefeller's company—or that she would

A journalist for a small newspaper interviews a member of the community.

pave the way for a change that would protect competition between businesses to this day.

Ida graduated from Allegheny College in 1880 with a biology degree, the only woman in her class. Unable to find a job as a biologist, she taught school for two years before joining the staff of the *Chautauqua Assembly Herald*. She reported for the *Herald* for six years, then left for France to write on her own. This decision, she later stated, took all the courage she possessed. Once in France, she began researching the life of Madame Philipon de Roland, her French Revolutionary heroine. Tarbell also sold stories of French life to American magazines. The quality of these articles led Samuel Sidney McClure to ask her to write for *McClure Magazine*.

McClure used his magazine as a forum to find solutions for problem issues of the day. He needed writers like Tarbell who were responsible and felt as he did about social injustice. Tarbell and McClure worked well together; he gave her job security and praise, while Tarbell in return gave him dedicated investigative reporting.

Tarbell gained added responsibilities at the magazine and was accepted and admired by her male colleagues. Paula Treckel, Professor of History at Allegheny College, relates in her article "The Business of Being a Woman" that Wytter Bynner, poetry editor at *McClure's* said Tarbell was as "firm as the Statue of Liberty . . . holding up the lantern of integrity."

Bynner recalled, "I can see her still, sitting there and gravely weighing prospects, possibilities, checking errors, smoothing differences. Her interest was mainly factual and moral rather than literary. . . . Every fiber of her was firm and true. . . . And this was not only in matters of magazine policy or contents. It was in personal matters too. She was pacifier and arbiter, philosopher and friend."

In the January 1903 issue of McClure's, Tarbell's first article on Rockefeller was printed. "The History of Standard Oil" showed how

John D. Rockefeller was one of the most powerful men of his day.

People who value justice and fairness:

- treat all people the same (as much as possible).
- are open-minded; they are willing to listen to the points of views others and try to understand.
- consider carefully before making decisions that affect others.
- don't take advantage of others' mistakes.
- don't take more than their fair share.
- cooperate with others.
- recognize the uniqueness and value of each individual.

Adapted from material from the Character Counts Coalition, charactercounts.org/overview/about.html

Rockefeller's illegal and unethical business practices destroyed competition in the oil industry. She wrote her article on Standard Oil like all her others, not as a criticism but rather an exposé. Her research was thorough and her evidence was strong. In the Standard Oil work, she uncovered how the *monopoly* was built. Presenting the facts in a just way was as important to Tarbell in this article as it was throughout her career.

Although Rockefeller was a powerful man, Tarbell did not fear him. He never answered any of her series of articles but remained silent, apparently hoping she would give up. Tarbell did not stop her inquiries, though, and her work strengthened the government's case against Standard Oil. Exposing plots to sidetrack rail cars, to interfere with rivals' shipments, and to pressure potential buyers to cancel orders, Tarbell shared how the oil company worked against smaller businesses. On November 15, 1906, South Improvement Company was charged with violating the Sherman Anti-Trust Act. The company was found guilty. Besides the breakup of the great oil monopoly, the Federal Trade Commission was also formed as a result of Tarbell's series. This commission was set up to protect competition between businesses in the hopes that such domination would not occur again.

How to Think More Fairly During the Reporting Process

Ask yourself these questions:

1. What do I know about this situation? Do I need to do something about what I know?
2. Why am I a journalist?
3. What are my ethical concerns?
4. How do I make my decisions? Should I follow any particular guidelines?
5. Do I consider others who may have different perspectives or ideas than my own when I am making a decision?
6. Who is affected by my decision?
7. What if the roles were reversed? How would I view my decision if I were the other person?
8. What are the possible consequences of my actions?
9. Am I telling the truth and being responsible? Am I causing any harm?
10. Am I justified in my decision to report this story? How will my family, colleagues, and the public feel about my decision?

Ida Tarbell worked hard as a journalist and embodied many of the traits persons of character value. Most of all, her sense of justice kept her focused and determined. Throughout her investigations, she admitted Rockefeller's amazing business sense, even though she felt the need to expose his injustices. Tarbell embodied the following elements of fairness and justice:

- She treated all people the same, recognizing their uniqueness.
- She remained open-minded and willing to understand another's position.

# 46

The Difference Between
Justice and Revenge

Justice wants what is fair.
Revenge wants to get even.

Justice sees both sides of the issue.
Revenge sees only from one perspective.

Justice seeks to bring healing and
peace.
Revenge continues a cycle of ever-
escalating violence.

- She weighed care-
fully the decisions
she made that would
affect others' lives.
- She didn't take ad-
vantage of others'
mistakes but merely
reported the truth,
whether good or
bad.

Anyone who values jus-
tice and fairness embraces
these same qualities.

For example, Doro-
thy Rabinowitz, who has
worked for the Wall Street
Journal since 1990, has
proven herself to be a writer who confronts tough issues fairly. She
is concerned with justice, and in 2001 she won the Pulitzer Prize in
commentary for her articles on American culture and society.

One of the injustices that Rabinowitz exposed occurred during
the trials of daycare workers accused of sexual abuse in the 1980s.
One such case was that of 60-year-old Violet Amirault, owner of the
Fells Acres Day School. Amirault, her daughter, Cheryl, and son
Gerald were accused of sexually abusing four- and five-year-olds
who attended their school. Rabinowitz studied the case and reported
her findings to the readers of the *Journal.*

When one hears of a child being abused, it is difficult to remain
unbiased, but Rabinowitz told the world a more objective story than
the one the media had reported at the time of the trials. In a series
of articles, she told of the Amiraults and others whose convictions of
such crimes were reversed when their cases were reviewed. Many of
the issues involved the children being "improperly influenced" by

other adults, which is a problem when young children are involved in issues such as these. The Amiraults all refused to plead guilty, even after the trial when they were in prison and offered favors, such as parole in return for a guilty plea. They consistently denied their guilt, and their insistence made others begin to question the Amiraults' conviction.

One of the jurors who served on the case wrote to Massachusetts Governor Paul Cellucci, asking that he release Gerald Amirault immediately (Violet and Cheryl had already been released by this time), stating that as he read more about the case in the newspapers, he was convinced of Gerald's innocence. Rabinowitz noted that the juror believed Gerald was wrongly convicted; his plea was for justice, not compassion. (In other words, he didn't simply feel sorry for Mr. Amirault.)

Rabinowitz visited the Amiraults while investigating their story, and she included in her articles her final visit with Violet only two days before Violet's death. Rabinowitz also appeared on a special panel at a Harvard Law School Conference, where she told those in attendance that the *Wall Street Journal* readers first learned of the Amiraults' story from her reports. She felt the facts told the truth themselves.

Without the facts, people believe what they hear from whoever tells their story, true or not, just or unjust. That's why journalists have such an important obligation to pursue justice in their work.

If you are considering journalism as a career, you should realize that this profession may sometimes put you in a position where you'll be asked to expose another's mistakes. Choosing what is right is always the best choice—but it may not always be the easiest one. Sometimes it's difficult to sort out our loyalties, our fears for our own reputation or safety, our personal anger or desire for revenge, and our commitment to justice.

Justice is a complicated issue, one that is sometimes confused with *retribution*. But the person of character demonstrates the sort of justice that is truly fair to everyone. This is the sort of fairness that Ida Tarbell and Dorothy Rabinowitz showed in their professional work—and journalists who today demonstrate justice like Tarbell's and Rabinowitz's continue to build a better world for each member of our society.

*If justice prevails, good faith is found in treaties, truth in transaction, order in government, the earth is at peace....*
                                        —Jacques Benique Bossuet

Peter Jennings has demonstrated his strong sense of responsibility throughout his long career.

# RESPONSIBILITY

*Being responsible every day—as well as
in a crisis—creates a world where
trust can grow.*

# CHAPTER FIVE

One of the most well known of all Canadian journalists was Peter Jennings, the former *anchor* and senior editor of ABC's *World News Tonight*. Jennings began working in his teens, for both radio and television. During his early 20s, he coanchored the late-night news. He was 25 when ABC hired him, and by age 26 he anchored the evening news. Only three years later, Jennings left this position to become a foreign correspondent. Some of his happiest memories are during the 15 years he spent overseas, including the time he covered Beirut and London. This is where he gained the international experience he relied on to report the news responsibly to his listeners.

Peter Jennings was an established part of **ABC**, until he passed away in 2005; he was an anchorman longer than anyone else. Jennings won the *Washington Journalism Review's* award for the country's best anchor for four years; he was given Harvard University's award for excellence in journalism, won dozens of Emmy awards, and more. His on-site filming locations included Sarajevo, the capital city of the Republic of Bosnia, and Herzegovina, where some of the most vicious fighting took place during the war from 1992 to 1995.

As a correspondent himself, Jennings valued the experience of other men and women who work in the field. He discussed how to approach a story so he was able to share what other reporters were experiencing. Taking the time to discover what was happening with correspondents was a large part of his responsibility for sharing

These journalists at a small newspaper may not have the same fame and prestige Peter Jennings had—but they too do their job responsibly.

accurate news. Jennings' international contacts supplied him with current news from their locations, as well as other points of view. Understanding what was happening from a native's view adds a more rounded dimension to the news. Jennings was serious about what stories got airtime. He would not run a story that he felt was inappropriate or unfair, and he took that responsibility seriously. He was also intensely involved in how the show appeared once it aired; he revised scripts at the last moment if he felt the change would make the program better for the viewers. His commitment showed in his long-standing anchoring career.

Jennings saw kindness to his colleagues as another of his responsibilities. For instance, Kevin Newman, also a Canadian broadcaster, received a phone call after someone critically reviewed him in a magazine article; the call was from Jennings, telling him not to worry about the unfavorable review because criticism like that happens to everyone in his position.

Kevin Newman is another Canadian-born journalist, one of the newest. Serving as a correspondent for ABC, Newman has appeared on *World News Tonight*, *Nightline*, and *Good Morning America*. A Toronto native, Newman began his broadcasting career in 1980 as a reporter for Global News, a Canadian television network. He also served as the network's parliamentary correspondent. Newman then

People who value responsibility:

- think before they act; they consider the possible consequences of their actions.
- accept responsibility for the consequences of their choices.
- don't blame others for their mistakes or take credit for others' achievements.
- don't make excuses.
- set a good example for others.
- pursue excellence in all they do.
- do the best with what they have.
- are dependable; others can rely on them.

Adapted from material from the Character Counts Coalition, charactercounts. org/overview/about.html

What motivates you (what's the "carrot" in your life?) to do your work responsibly?

moved to the Canadian Broadcasting Corporation (CBC) in the same capacity, with an emphasis on foreign affairs and defense issues. For two years he served as an anchor of *Midday*, the Canadian daily, hour-long news program, as well as substitute anchor for two major evening news programs.

In 1994, Newman was hired by ABC to anchor *World News This Morning* and *World News Now*.

He then became a correspondent in 1996 for ABC's *World News Tonight* with Peter Jennings. From there he moved to *Good Morning America*. He spent nine years anchoring *Global National*, followed by a move to *CTV National News in Canada*.

Jennings never lost his concern for Canadian news, and lobbied for Canadian coverage. He was given the golden key award by the City of Ottawa and considered it an honor. He also owned a farm in Quebec's Gatineau Hills where he enjoyed vacations and weekends.

### The Canadian Association of Journalists (CAJ)

The mission statement of the CAJ states that it promotes excellence in journalism and encourages investigative journalism. The association is the national voice of Canadian journalists; it preserves the public's right to know the news.

The CAJ' s goals are:

- To continue to build on the professional development foundation laid by more than 20 years of national conferences, awards, and writers' symposia.
- To provide members with network, advocacy and information services.
- To encourage grass roots growth by encouraging regional and chapter activity.
- To provide insight into the world of journalism and tools of the trade through Media Magazine, a quarterly publication.
- To partner with other journalism, advocacy, or professional development organizations who share similar goals and beliefs.

From www.caj.ca

Attention to detail, commitment to quality, and dependable work are all parts of this journalist's job.

Newman's calm, responsible manner while covering Princess Diana's death in 1997 futhered his career. His reporting was respectful and disciplined. Listeners received the facts in a timely fashion rather than being misled by stories that had not actually happened. Newman also took responsibility for the behind-the-scenes coverage that night, another example of his commitment to his profession and those he served. A crisis is always a situation where people reveal their true characters. For Newman, the test proved successful.

Since his career puts him in the eyes of the public, Newman has had to become aware of the image he needs to portray. Image is an integral part of public news broadcasting, so Newman has had to change his clothing choices slightly and begin wearing contacts instead of glasses. He insists, however, that although he will learn what is necessary for his job he will not change who he is inside. The same ethics and morals that made him responsible and respectful during the Princess Diana broadcasts are those he embodies throughout his journalistic career.

Both Jennings and Newman have shown their sense of responsibility while performing their jobs. Being dependable and performing their best are challenges journalists face daily. They accept their obligations to those they work with and to those they work for. Their sense of responsibility to their colleagues, listeners, and readers inspires them to do their best.

Nothing we do ever stands by itself. If it is good, it will serve some good purpose in the future.

—Eleanor Roosevelt

Reporter Terry Anderson had the courage to endure kidnapping.

# COURAGE

*Being responsible every day—as well as
in a crisis—creates a world where
trust can grow.*

# CHAPTER SIX

On March 16, 1985, Terry Anderson dropped off a friend after a tennis game. Within minutes he found himself in the back seat of a green Mercedes, covered with a blanket, and traveling through the streets of Moslem West Beirut. At the time of his abduction, Anderson was the chief Middle East correspondent for the Associated Press (AP). His passion for journalism and his love for Beirut combined to put him in a position of danger in a country not always welcoming to those who seek the truth.

Working as an eyewitness reporter meant taking risks. Others like him face similar dangers around the world. For Anderson the trip in the green Mercedes began a seven-year prison sentence. He

Terry Anderson is interviewed by fellow journalist Ted Koppel.

endured beatings, humiliations, and vile food in tiny, dark underground cells. Anderson had been kidnapped by the Iranian-backed Hezbollah, who claimed to have taken Anderson and others in a continuing effort against America and its agents; the Shi'i Muslims belonging to Hezbollah wanted to rid Lebanon of all Americans. Their retaliation for Israel's 1982 invasion of Lebanon was the beginning of the campaign that eventually forced Americans to leave their country.

Not alone in his ordeal, Anderson became a brave leader for his fellow hostages. He insisted on a clean cell. He made a

People who value courage:

- say what's right (even when no one agrees with them).
- do the right thing (even when it's hard).
- follow their conscience instead of the crowd.

deck of cards from bits of paper and then a chess set from scraps of aluminum foil. He darned the same pair of socks over and over throughout his imprisonment and mended others' clothes as well. As he encouraged the other prisoners, Anderson helped himself. He felt a great need for their companionship, and he especially enjoyed being able to talk to them of intellectual things. He wanted to feel as if he still belonged to the real world, and he drew courage from the support of his fellow prisoners.

Thomas Sutherland, a dean at the American University of

Journalists continue to face the possibility of being kidnapped during conflicts in the Middle East today. Olaf Wiig, a New Zealand photojournalist, and Steve Centanni, an American reporter, were kidnapped in the Gaza Strip in 2006. They were released after two weeks. Four *New York Times* journalists were kidnapped in Libya in 2011, and released a few days later. One had already been kidnapped a few years earlier. *New York Times* journalist David Rohde was kidnapped by the Taliban in Afghanistan in 2008. He managed to escape from captivity in 2009.

Arthur Kent reported courageously on the violence in Afghanistan.

On October 23, 1983, Terry Anderson's article about the suicide bombing in Beirut, Lebanon told of the truck filled with explosives that drove into a four-story building where United States Marines slept. Seventy-six Marines were killed and 115 were wounded. Moments later another truck drove into a multinational compound, killing as many as 100 French soldiers. Anderson told of the destruction, the digging efforts to free trapped soldiers, and of ambulances and helicopters used in efforts to get help to those still alive.

Journalists' jobs often take them to the most dangerous "hot spots" of the world.

The Gospels in the Christian New Testament are journalistic accounts that changed the world forever.

Beirut, was his cellmate for much of his captivity; most of that time they were chained together. Sutherland taught Anderson French from a historical text given to them by the guards. They also made elaborate plans for a dairy farm, including budgeting all the expenses. Sutherland said after his release that he could not have endured captivity for six and a half years without Anderson and his courage to keep contemplating different subjects.

Taking risks has been a large part of Canadian journalist Arthur Kent's career. He needed courage to report from the conflict zones in Afghanistan and Bosnia. He was on a Saudi Arabian rooftop in 1991, where he witnessed the beginning of the Gulf War. From the former Soviet Union to China, Kent's factual style of reporting encompassed solo filming

Journalism is a career that can have a profound impact on human society. Matthew, Mark, Luke, and John were early journalists who recorded the life story of Jesus Christ. Their reports, contained in the Gospels of the Christian New Testament, not only changed the entire world, but they continue to inspire millions of people. Journalists with courage have the same power today.

expeditions, as well as being a member of large network teams. His independent films, *A View of Bosnia* (1993), *Return to Afghanistan* (1995), and *A Wedding in Basra* (1998), received several awards and honors from film festivals and human-rights groups in Canada and the United States.

He has taken on another challenge as well, summoning a courage different from that needed in crises: Kent is trying to make others aware of the need to bring ethics back to the business of journalism. In his book, *Risk and Redemption: Surveying the Network Wars*, Kent studied the issue of ethics in the media. He has begun a fight for greater standards in reporting, since he feels in many cases large companies who run broadcasting are making decisions about the news based on money rather than the truth. In his book, Kent tackled some important questions like: What happens when ratings become more important than the pursuit of truth? And why would standard news coverage be sacrificed for entertainment-oriented magazine shows?

Kent speaks out about the changes in broadcasting. He insists that the quest for ratings many times outweighs the traditional editorial ideals of broadcast news. He argues that sensationalism has replaced restraint. And he feels strongly about the need for a balance between domestic and foreign coverage. In his article "Bringing Down the Barriers," Kent explains that the people who are the conscience of broadcast news are the working journalists. But they have less and less influence on what appears on the daily news. Speaking out may bring negative consequences professionally, but Kent feels if journalists do not have the courage to do so, broadcast news may not survive.

Courage shows itself in different ways. For Terry Anderson, courage enabled him to face danger with a resolution to withstand whatever trials he faced. He not only showed strength for himself, though; he affected those who were imprisoned with him. Arthur Kent showed courage by confronting journalists and challenging them to resist changes that lead them away from basic values.

Doing the right thing is not always easy. But without reporters like Terry Anderson and Arthur Kent, free countries would be unable to hear the truth behind world happenings. Reports would come to readers and listeners *biased* toward the side of whoever wanted to proclaim a *subjective* viewpoint. Anderson's and Kent's brave journalism continues to be a challenge to news reporters throughout the world—and their personal courage inspires us all.

---

*A vast deal may be done by those who dare to act.*

—Jane Austen

---

Robert Woodward and Carl Bernstein had the self-discipline and diligence to stick with one of the most important stories of the century.

# SELF-DISCIPLINE AND DILIGENCE

*When others don't believe in what you're doing, only self-discipline and diligence can keep you going.*

# CHAPTER SEVEN

On June 17, 1972, five men were found breaking into the Democratic Headquarters in the Watergate Hotel and apartment complex. For the two young reporters from the *Washington Post* who investigated the Watergate break-in, life would never be the same. Because of the information that Robert Upshur Woodward and Carl Bernstein uncovered, the entire United States would never be the same either.

Although many felt the break-in was not newsworthy, Woodward and Bernstein wondered about the connection between the burglars and President Nixon's reelection committee. The two jour-

People who value self-discipline and diligence:

- work to control their emotions, words, actions, and impulses.
- give their best in all situations.
- keep going even when the going is rough.
- are determined and patient.
- try again even when they fail the first time.
- look for ways to do their work better.

Adapted from material from the Character Education Network (www.CharacterEd.Net).

nalists wanted more information. Each bit of evidence led to something more, and they realized that each step took them closer to the Republican Party leaders. From their first article to their last, the two reporters investigated what had happened piece by piece. Because of the nature of their exposés, their sources had to be painstakingly checked and authenticated.

The *Post* was the only paper publishing stories about Watergate when the deception began, and Woodward and Bernstein continued to probe alone into the facts. Not having any fellow journalists working on the story forced them to work harder to collect information. Others in the news world criticized the *Post* for carrying Woodward and Bernstein's reports, but the newspaper continued to print Woodward and Bernstein's stories.

Finally, near the end of October 1972, Walter Cronkite broadcast two consecutive nights on Watergate. This brought the situation more coverage and during the winter of 1972–73, other editors became interested in the Watergate story. At last, other investigative journalists joined Woodward and Bernstein in their quest for the truth.

But people were still not convinced Watergate was a story worthy of attention. Many popular politicians thought the reporters were ruining their newspaper by giving coverage to the scandal. But

President Richard Nixon's involvement with the Watergate scandal led to his resignation.

Woodward and Bernstein did not turn away from the challenge that faced them. They were diligent before they even knew they were working on the story of a lifetime. Their self-discipline as they asked questions, more questions, and even more questions allowed them to gain information, even if it was only one small piece at a time. But the pieces kept fitting together and leading on to others, including a *slush fund* used to investigate and discredit Democratic politicians, the discovery of the "plumbers" who were ordered to plug leaks in the administration, and the possibility of tapes recorded by President Nixon throughout the incident.

An anonymous contact became known as Deep Throat. He supplied Woodward and Bernstein with enough infor-

If you doubt you can accomplish something, then you can't accomplish it. You have to have confidence in your ability, and then be tough enough to follow through.
—Rosalynn Carter

Journalists need diligence and self-discipline to work the long hours necessary to meet deadlines.

mation to keep them going forward. Deep Throat assured them there was more to the break-in than seemed to be the case. With his prompting, the investigation finally led to the White House.

During the Senate Watergate hearings, the Nixon tapes became public knowledge. These tapes provided proof that President Nixon was involved in the scandal. This climax did not happen until August of 1974, when Woodward and Bernstein had followed the story for more than two years. By then, the *Post* had published more than 300 Watergate stories. Woodward and Bernstein had worked hard and endured long hours; now it looked like the end was in sight. The *Post* made a decision to give no interviews in connection with the resolution. No one was to act in any way like they were happy or boasting about the outcome. The President resigned and it was over.

But the effects have been far reaching. Because of Watergate, the government has made an effort to reform campaigns. Some of these reforms include the Federal Election Commission improvement that requires political parties to regularly submit a list of their

Because of Woodward and Bernstein's diligent journalism, Americans hold the White House accountable in new ways.

contributors. There were also reforms that control mail sent to constituents at taxpayers' expense. Slush funds like the one used by the White House were eliminated. And the amounts used to fund elections are limited at each government level.

If not for the persistence of Woodward and Bernstein, the Watergate story might have been a different one. Their diligence and self-discipline gave them the strength they needed to commit themselves to one story. They never revealed Deep Throat's name, and his identity remained a secret until 2005, when it was revealed that Deep Throat was Mark Felt, a former Associate Director of the FBI. Their determination and discipline meant they kept going even when others were against them—and they continue to do so today.

Do you have that kind of self-discipline and diligence?

*Most of the important things in the world have been accomplished by people who have kept on trying when there seemed to be no hope at all.*

—Herbert Meyer

Because of the words and pictures sent to us by journalists, we can better grasp the fact that we belong to the same human community as this Afghan woman and her baby.

# CITIZENSHIP

*Sometimes being a good citizen means you are loyal to your nation or local community—and sometimes it means your highest loyalties belong to the Earth's entire human community.*

# CHAPTER EIGHT

Dexter Filkins is one of the reporters who has covered the "War on Terror" in both Afghanistan and Iraq following the September 11, 2001 attack on the Twin Towers and the Pentagon. Working as a news correspondent in foreign countries, Dexter Filkins reports on things he sees and finds while living amid the turmoil of areas where he is at risk each day he does his job.

Filkins worked for several years as a foreign correspondent for the *New York Times*, ever since 2001. Over eight years of reporting, he collected enough information to write a book, *The Forever War*, which describes the war in often terrifying detail. He has been a

Reporters like Dexter Filkins report on political conflict around the world, including the events in Afghanistan after the terrorist attacks on the United States in 2001.

finalist for the Pulitzer Prize twice, and has won several prestigious journalism prizes.

Filkins' writing focuses on what war actually looks like, and how it affects those living in the warzone. He writes about ordinary people, from Afghans to Iraqis to American soldiers. He treats his subjects as human beings, and allows readers in other countries to understand war from a different point of view. In *The Forever War*, he writes, "Iraq might have been a traumatized country, it might have been broken, it might have been atomized.... But whenever the prospect of normalcy presented itself, a long line of Iraqis always stood up and reached for it."

Like many other journalists working in dangerous situations, Filkins knows he must be careful. Many journalists are not prepared to face the harsh realities of a war, or to tell the stories of people living through it. Dexter has seen a lot of violence, and has reported on everything from government corruption to suicide bombings. He told National Public Radio, "It's incredibly dangerous.... The level of violence in Helmand and Kandahar in southern Afghanistan...has really, really risen as the troops have gone into the areas where frankly, they haven't been before. So they're having to fight their way into these areas. So it's become extremely difficult for us to cover. We still do. But it's just at much greater risk." Despite that risk, Filkins' dedication to the truth has kept him moving from one hot spot to another.

Dexter Filkins can be trusted to tell what is happening, exactly as it happens, in an unbiased way that considers equally all those involved. Filkins is just and fair and shows respect and compassion for those whose stories he tells. Through his journalism, he puts character qualities to work for the benefit of the entire human community.

However, not all journalists are always honest. Jack Kelley, a respected foreign correspondent much like Filkins, was found to have lied and fabricated many of his stories. He was even a finalist for the Pulitzer Prize in 2002. Two years later, *USA Today* conducted an

People who value citizenship:

- play by the rules.
- obey the law.
- do their share.
- respect authority.
- stay informed about current events.
- vote.
- protect their neighbors and community.
- pay their taxes.
- give to others in their community who are in need.
- volunteer to help.
- protect the environment.
- conserve natural resources for the future.

Adapted from material from the Character Counts Coalition, charactercounts.org/overview/about.html

investigation of his reporting, and concluded that he had purposefully made up information for his stories.

Most journalists know that understanding all sides of the truth and reporting it in an unbiased way allows others in the world to better understand those who are different from them. And those who understand better may be able to help bring about positive change.

Some people believe citizenship equals patriotism. But we are all citizens of the entire world, and we cannot cut ourselves off

I've always wanted to help people in some way. As an investigative reporter, I am able to dig up the information people want to know and expose those who try to take advantage of others. At the end of the day, I want to go home knowing I have made a difference.

—Lechelle Yates, Investigative Reporter

Citizenship may mean loyalty to our own nation—but it may also ask us to extend our loyalties beyond our own nation and consider what is best for all the people of the world.

Investigative Reporters and Editors, Inc. (IRE) is a grassroots nonprofit organization dedicated to improving the quality of investigative reporting. The IRE was formed in 1975 to create a forum in which journalists throughout the world could help each other by sharing story ideas, newsgathering techniques and news sources.

from those who live in other nations. What affects people on the other side of the world will ultimately affect each of us as well, for our world is interconnected. Journalists like Dexter Filkins who are loyal to the truth are powerful citizens of the worldwide human community. Their citizenship builds a foundation for a more peaceful world.

*If we want to make something really superb of our community and this planet, nothing whatever can stop us.*

—Shepherd Mead

Reporters have the opportunity to expose the truth about poverty and other painful realities.

# CAREER
# OPPORTUNITIES

*Journalists have many opportunities from
which to choose—but all offer the chance
to make a difference in our world.*

# CHAPTER NINE

A n immigrant himself, Jacob Riis worked for reform in New
York City for the thousands of immigrants living there. His
book *How the Other Half Lives* is a photo documentary of
the lives of those immigrants. The information Riis shared about
life in the 2.76 acres of Mulberry Bend helped bring about needed
changes. Theodore Roosevelt called Riis "the most useful citizen of
New York."

Using a newly developed handheld camera and a flash-gun, Riis
photographed the misery he beheld in the crowded, poverty-ridden

Beginning reporters cover court proceedings and civic and club meetings, summarize speeches, and write obituaries. With experience, they report more difficult assignments, cover an assigned beat, or specialize in a particular field.

*tenements* and lodging houses of the mid-1880s. He took pictures because he was sure words could not describe what he witnessed.

Riis's images of the deplorable conditions of immigrants and their children shocked his readers. Politicians and others forced lodging houses to close, lights were mounted in tenement hallways, and the city

Jacob Riis used his camera to tell a heartbreaking story; his courage and integrity brought about positive changes.

provided a clean water supply. Riis used his ability to report accurately the abuses most New Yorkers did not witness. Until they read his stories, wealthy citizens of the city did not see the loss of health and lives; the death rate of children under five in Mulberry Bend was about one out of seven. Once New Yorkers were aware of the situation, however, they forced those who gained financially from this squalor to change or leave.

Considered one of the founders of documentary photography, Riis used his camera in a strictly utilitarian way. "I had a use for it," Riis wrote of the camera, "and beyond that I never went." Printing at the time necessitated wood engravings that reduced the details of the prints, but the pictures still showed poverty and squalor all too clearly.

Today photographic journalists are often self-employed. They offer photographs and articles to magazines that accept freelance submissions. Photojournalists make up a small percent of those employed in the field.

Salaries for journalists vary widely, but, in general, are only slightly higher than the average salary for all U.S. workers. Median annual earnings of reporters, correspondents, and broadcast news analysts was $36,000 in 2010. Broadcast news analysts earned more, with an average of $54,140. The highest paid broadcast news analysts earned more than $146,200. Reporters and correspondents earned an average of $34,530.

From U.S. Department of Labor's Occupational Outlook Handbook, www.bls.gov/ooh

As a journalist, you will have many opportunities from which to choose.

Every year, the James M. Cox Jr. Center for International Mass Communication Training and Research conducts a survey of recent graduates in journalism fields. Here's some of what the center found in 2011:

- 62.2% of bachelor's degree recipients had full-time employment five months after graduation.

- the salaries of 2011 graduates were slightly higher than they had been a year before.

- 2011 graduates had an average of 1.4 job offers when they graduated.

According to the Society of Professional Journalists Code of Ethics, journalists should:

- Clarify and explain news coverage and invite dialogue with the public over journalistic conduct.
- Encourage the public to voice grievances against the news media.
- Admit mistakes and correct them properly.
- Expose unethical practices of journalists and the news media.
- Abide by the same high standards to which they hold others.

Nearly half of all journalists work for newspapers, either large city dailies or suburban and small town dailies or weeklies. About 26 percent work in radio and television broadcasting, magazines, and wire services. News analysts, reporters, and correspondents that are self-employed represent another 25 percent of the field.

The employment outlook is in decline for news reporters and correspondents, although growth is expected in employment of broadcast news analysts. Many news organizations have consolidated, and have cut costs by reducing the number of reporters and correspondents they employ. As fewer people read newspapers, watch the news on TV, or listen to it on the radio, newspapers and television and radio stations have less need for journalists.

However, writers who specialize in fields such as science or technical subjects have an advantage. Most journalists, however, begin working at a small publication or a small-town or suburban newspaper as a way to gain experience and credentials. Some journalists work in advertising or public relations. Because economic ups and downs affect newspaper and broadcasting industries, openings in the field fluctuate.

Journalists face many challenges—and many exciting opportunities as well.

Some news analysts and reporters can advance by moving to large newspapers or television stations. A few experienced reporters become columnists, correspondents, writers, announcers, or public relations specialists. Others become editors in print journalism or program managers in broadcast journalism, who supervise reporters. Some eventually become broadcasting or publications industry managers.

Working hours vary for most reporters. Many newspaper reporters work early mornings or late nights, depending on when their newspapers must be ready for delivery. Deadlines like these create pressure and many times the work must be done in large rooms filled with the sounds of other employees accomplishing their work. Television or radio reporters are usually assigned a day or evening shift. If there is special news to cover, working hours become longer. Investigative reporters who cover wars, political uprisings, fires, or floods often travel to distant places and may sometimes face great danger.

Working as a journalist can be a rewarding experience and a fulfilling career. Some essential points to remember include:

- Jobs often are stressful because of irregular hours, frequent night and weekend work, and pressure to meet deadlines— but the opportunities for adventure and excitement are good.
- Those journalists who believe character plays an important role in society are able to influence ethical thinking with what they write.
- Journalists throughout history have played major roles in changing the world for the better—and even small areas of change can make a significant difference in the lives of those affected.

If you are interested in a career as a journalist, remember that education and training are important. You can look forward to advancements and salary increases if you work hard at your profession. But more important, as a journalist you have the power to encourage the qualities of character: integrity, compassion, justice, responsibility, courage, diligence, and citizenship.

*If you don't like the way the world is, you change it. You have an obligation to change it.*

—Marian Wright Edelman

# Further Reading

Anderson, Terry. *Den of Lions: Memoir of Seven Years*. New York: Ballantine, 1995.

Bernstein, Carl and Bob Woodward. *The Final Days*. New York: Simon and Schuster, 2005.

Briggs, Mark. *Journalism Next: A Practical Guide to Digital Reporting and Publishing*. Washington, D.C.: CQ Press, 2009.

Ferguson, Donald L., Jim Patten, and Morley Safer. *Opportunities in Journalism Careers*. Lincolnwood, Ill.: McGraw-Hill, 2001.

Fradin, Dennis Brindell, Judith Bloom Fradin. *Ida B. Wells: Mother of the Civil Rights Movement*. New York: Clarion Books, 2000.

Josephson, Michael S. and Wes Hanson, editors. *The Power of Character*. Bloomington, Ind.: Unlimited Press, 2004.

Kidder, Rushworth M. *How Good People Make Tough Choices*. New York: HarperCollins, 2009.

Riis, Jacob A. *How the Other Half Lives*. New York: Dover Publishing, 1991.

# For More Information

American Booksellers Association
www.ambook.org

American Society of Journalists and Authors
www.asja.org/index.php

American Society of Newspaper Editors Foundation
www.asne.org

Canadian Society of Children's Authors,
Illustrators, and Performers
www.canscaip.org

Center for the Study of Ethics in Professions
www.iit.edu/departments/csep

Indiana School of Journalism Ethics
www.journalism.indiana.edu/Ethics

Magazine Publishers of America
www.magazine.org

Society of Children's Writers and Illustrators
www.scbwi.org

Writers Guild of America
www.wgaeast.org and www.wga.org

Writers Union of Canada
www.writersunion.ca

Publisher's Note:
The websites on this page were active at the time of publication. The publisher is not responsible for websites that have changed their address or discontinued operation since the date of publication. The publisher will review and update the websites upon each reprint.

# Glossary

*Anchor*   A broadcaster who introduces other broadcasters and reads the main news.

*Biased*   Having a slanted viewpoint; seeing from one perspective only.

*Copyediting*   Revising, correcting errors, and creating headlines for a newspaper.

*Ethics*   The study of what is right and wrong.

*Freelance writer*   A writer who is self-employed.

*Ghostwriter*   A writer who creates a book or article under someone else's name.

*Monopoly*   When a single organization controls all aspects of a particular business.

*Propaganda*   "News" that has been manipulated to support a particular cause or to hurt an opposing cause, which is spread as fact when it may be exaggerated or completely fabricated.

*Retribution*   Punishment.

*Slush fund*   Money used for bribing officials or for propaganda.

*Stringer*   A part-time news reporter who is paid according to the amount of space filled by his or her article, rather than a salary.

*Subjective*   Having to do with an individual's own self-focused point of view.

*Tenements*   Apartment buildings lacking adequate safety and sanitation measures.

# Index

# About the Author & Consultants

Sherry Bonnice lives with her husband and two children on a dirt road in rural Pennsylvania. They raise rabbits and have a small farm with a goat, a sheep, chickens, one duck, five dogs, and two cats. Sherry has co-edited quilt magazines and written a quilt book. She has also written several books for other Mason Crest series, including Careers with Character and North American Folklore.

Cheryl Gholar is a Community and Economic Development Educator with the University of Illinois Extension. She has a Ph.D. in Educational Leadership and Policy Studies from Loyola University, and she has more than 20 years of experience with the Chicago Public Schools as a teacher, counselor, guidance coordinator, and administrator. Recognized for her expertise in the field of character education, Dr. Gholar assisted in developing the K–12 Character Education Curriculum for the Chicago Public Schools, and she is a five-year participant in the White House Conference on Character Building for a Democratic and Civil Society. The recipient of numerous awards, she is also the author of Beyond Rhetoric and Rainbows: A Journey to the Place Where Learning Lives.

Ernestine G. Riggs is an Assistant Professor at Loyola University Chicago and a Senior Program Consultant for the North Central Regional Educational Laboratory. She has a Ph.D. in Educational Leadership and Policy Studies from Loyola University, and she has been involved in the field of education for more than 35 years. An advocate of teaching the whole child, she is a frequent presenter at district and national conferences; she also serves as a consultant for several state boards of education. Dr. Riggs has received many citations, including an award from the United States Department of Defense Overseas Schools for Outstanding Elementary Teacher of America.